MW01002568

A Study Guide

To Love

&

To Be Loved

Establishing
Healthy Relationships

Lisa L. Schwarz

The Study Guide for To Love and To Be Loved:
Establishing Healthy Relationships
ISBN-13: 978-1722433017
Copyright © 2018 Lisa L. Schwarz

Contact the author:

Lisa Schwarz
831 Evergreen Lane
Burleson, TX 76028
www.Lisa-Schwarz.com
www.Crazy8Ministries.com

Accompanying book by Lisa L. Schwarz: *To Love & To Be Loved*
ISBN: 978-1-978480-31-5

Preface

This workbook was written for the purpose of helping you maximize the concepts in the book, *To Love and To Be Loved: Establishing Healthy Relationships.* It is my desire to help you do more than simply gain information from the book, but rather to learn how to take that information and turn it into action in a way that will transform your relationships.

ENGAGE, REFLECT & PERSONALIZE

With each chapter, there are questions that will help you to engage with the concept by reflecting and personalizing what is being presented. The purpose is to train you to do more than gain information, but to consider how that information is relevant in your own life and how it can transform your mind more into the mind of Christ.

EXECUTE

Each chapter also has a section to teach you how to take information and execute it through action. This is how we learn to "train ourselves toward righteousness."

Every nugget of information or revelation that God brings is an invitation to respond through action.

As with life, the more you put into this, the more you will get out of it! I like to tell my personal clients that when they think they are done with an assignment, to go back and press into it another layer. Be intentional to ask (with expectation) the Holy Spirit to show you more and take it deeper. This practice will often shift you from soul answers to spirit answers.

I pray that this workbook equips you to move beyond good relationships to GREAT relationships. May you come to embrace God's design for your relationships and be equipped and empowered to enforce that design. May you love more deeply and be loved more freely as you step out into the depths of HIS design for love!

A Study Guide: To Love & To Be Loved

RELATIONSHIP QUIZ

Before we get started with this study guide, take a moment to quickly assess your current relationships. Take some time to consider specific relationships within the areas of family, friends and romance. This may require you doing the quiz multiple times within each section.

Rate each statement on a scale of 1-10...10 being an "Absolute yes!"

____ I feel physically safe.
____ I feel emotionally safe and feel free to be vulnerable.
____ I feel free to be transparent and honest.
____ I feel free to say no.
____ I feel to give my opinion... even when I disagree.
____ I feel generally satisfied and fulfilled.
____ I feel celebrated.
____ There is no jealousy.
____ I can openly communicate without fear of judgment or ridicule.
____ There is mutual care and I don't feel taken advantage of.
____ There is mutual ownership of wrongs and a general sense of humility.

10 points being possible for all ten statements makes 100 the potential. If you scored anything less that 100 in any of your relationships, it is possible that you are experiencing less than God's best for you in the area of

healthy connections. It was important to honestly evaluate where you are in your relationships in order to consider that God may have more for you!

Use this list as a mental checklist as you move forward in your relationships along with the empowerment of the book to ensure that you are enforcing God's design for relationships in your life. Don't settle for less than HIS best!

A Study Guide: To Love & To Be Loved

SECTION 1

UNDERSTANDING HEALTHY RELATIONSHIPS

Read the introduction and Chapter 1

ENGAGE, REFLECT & PERSONALIZE:

After reading through the introduction, how would you say that your relationships have affected your quality of life? Be specific and be willing to list relationships that have helped you prosper and relationships that have held you back.

_____
_____
_____
_____
_____

Think of people in your life that you would say have unhealthy relationships, and some that have healthy relationships. Do you see any correlation to how they prosper or "move ahead" in their lives?

After reading through Chapter 1, would you say that you have a strong connection with people? Why or why not? How does the idea of being transparent or vulnerable come into play with those connections, or lack there of?

_____

_____

_____

_____

Would you say that you tend be a transparent person? Why or why not? In the places where you feel free to be transparent (if any), what is it that gives you that permission to be completely free?

_____

_____

_____

_____

Do you think others would say they feel free to be "real" with you? Are you intentional to cultivate that type of freedom within your relationships? Why is that important?

_____

_____

_____

_____

God wants to connect with you in your most vulnerable places. How does this Truth impact your idea of connecting more intimately with God and how can it bring about more freedom in your walk with Him? Do you sense any fear in this?

_____

_____

_____

_____

_____

EXECUTE:

Take some time to reflect on times when you felt closest or most connected with God. What was happening at that time in your life? Would you say that it was a place of vulnerability for you? Take a moment to thank God for connecting with you in those moments and for intensifying His intimacy through them.

Now, resolve to consider this exercise at the end of each day for the next week. Every day brings about moments of vulnerability or insecurity...these are opportunities to intentionally be transparent with God about what you are experiencing. Fear will try to keep you from pressing in and will tell you to avoid it or run from it. However, we must attack fear by training ourselves to "let God in" to our most difficult places! Remember, He is standing at the door of your heart continually knocking on every door that it holds so that He can connect with you behind each one!

PART 1: DEFINING RELATIONSHIPS

Read Chapters 2 and 3

ENGAGE, REFLECT & PERSONALIZE:

After reading about God's design of a healthy relationship, which trait or traits do you feel stood out the most to you and why? Did this list change the way you look at your current relationships? Why or why not?

_____
_____
_____
_____

After reading about the many forms of unhealthy relationships, which one or ones do you feel stood out the most to you and why? Did this list change the way you look at your relationships? Why or Why not?

_____
_____
_____
_____

In your own words, describe how fear cultivates unhealthy relationships.

_____
_____
_____
_____
_____

A Study Guide: To Love & To Be Loved

Through the descriptions, did the Holy Spirit illuminate any fear within your relationships? If so, how do you feel Him challenging you in regard?

_____
_____
_____
_____
_____

Did you become aware of any unhealthy traits that you operate in within your relationships (other than fear)... like manipulation, co-dependency, etc.? If so, why do you think God is allowing you to recognize that?

_____
_____
_____
_____
_____

EXECUTE:

Take some time to reflect on areas in your relationships where you operate in fear. Confess that fear to God and repent of it...handing it over for Him to heal. Then, pray through and declare 1 John 4:18 over your own heart and mind. Here is an example:

"God I thank You that in You I find a perfect love and that by Your love all fear is gone. I receive Your love and agree that with You, I have no fear. I confess that fear of man has dominated the security I find in Your perfect love and I declare that today Your love is overtaking all my fears."

Also, take time to be intentional to confess to God any other unhealthy trait that you identified above. Recognize how the root of them is fear. Ask the Holy Spirit to open your eyes to when you are operating in these tendencies so that you will become "sensitive" to them and how they are rooted in fear. Once you notice them, go back to 1 John 4:18 and the prayer example above.

PART 2: REDEFINING RELATIONSHIPS

Read Chapter 4

ENGAGE, REFLECT & PERSONALIZE:

How does knowing that you played a part in the establishment of the "personality" of each of your current relationships empower you? How does that give you hope as you consider making changes?

_____

_____

_____

_____

Take a moment to consider any unhealthy relationships you may have. Would you say they are simply difficult, disappointing, or destructive? How does categorizing them help alter your mindset in regard?

_____

_____

_____

_____

What specific patterns of YOUR behavior helped mold your relationships? Would you say those patterns line up with the patterns of Jesus? Can you identify any personality tendencies you have that are NOT in the likeness of Christ? In other words, what tendencies do you have that are based on your own pattern, or the pattern of your system, rather than on the tendencies of Jesus?

_____

_____

_____

_____

How do you tend to be affected by the behavior of others? How did the understanding or mirroring spirits enlighten you in regard?

_____

_____

_____

_____

EXECUTE:

James says that our soul, or our personality is rescued or sanctified by the washing of the Word or the implantation of it. (John 17:17 and James 1:21) This means that in order to transform our current patterns, we must retrain our minds through the Word of God. After identifying patterns that you have that do NOT look like Christ, look up verses that directly counter that pattern. Then read through those verses and ask how you can change your behaviors, responses, or words to look more like what Scripture is teaching you.

This is the process of "training yourself toward righteousness." Remember, this may seem...or actually may be simply mechanical at first...but any new thing is.

But, as you operate on faith based on the Word, God will sanctify your heart and your mind. We can change our behavior, but only God can change the heart! BUT...that transformation is activated by our faith displayed in action.

Read Chapter 5

ENGAGE, REFLECT & PERSONALIZE:

In your own words, what would you say is the purpose of boundaries? Can you think of specific ways that boundaries have helped mold you into who you are today? Can you think of specific ways that LACK of boundaries has helped mold you into who you are today?

_____
_____
_____
_____

Consider your "lot" and the "lots" of those around you. What would you say is the main reason you tend to jump into other people's "lots"? How about why you let others inside your "lot?" Do you see where there may be fear involved in both cases? What would you identify as you fear?

_____
_____
_____
_____

What do you think is the hardest for you in regard to setting boundaries? Why?

_____
_____
_____
_____
_____

EXECUTE:

Identify one relationship where you know you need to set some boundaries. Write down why you think you need boundaries. Does your why line up with God's design for you? It is important that you are guarding your design along with the other person's design in mind as well.

Assuming your need for boundaries is in line with God, play out in your mind the moments when a boundary would be healthy, and what would that boundary look like? Prepare BEFORE you are in the moment while your emotions are NOT in play. This is important!! Pray and invite God into the process as you play it over in your mind and allow HIS love to empower your boundary. Then ask God to show you a doable consequence for, if and when, your boundary is crossed, dismissed or disrespected. Again, this must be decided ahead of time to ensure that it is an intentional decision that has been led by the Holy Spirit.

Consider this process in reverse. Ask the Holy Spirit to reveal any places where you may be squelching or simply not appreciating the design of someone else in your life. Are there places where you control, manipulate, or operate in fear that ends up keeping anyone else from living up to their full purpose? Open your heart up to God and allow Him to probe...be willing to see things from HIS perspective. Because of our system, most of us often have some of these tendencies that are rooted in fear of not being loved. It is important that as you set boundaries for your own life that you consider where you need to stop infringing on the boundaries of those around you.

A Study Guide: To Love & To Be Loved

PERSONAL REFLECTION

Before we move on to section 2, take time to reflect on these questions. The goal here is to help you self discover you...and the way you give and receive love.

Which do you personally find easier...loving or being loved? Why? Do you think it has anything to do with the way you were raised or the "culture" that helped define love/in other words, your family?

_____

_____

_____

_____

How would you say the world defines love? How would you say religion defines love? How do you define love?

_____

_____

_____

_____

_____

How do you best show love? How do you best receive love? What makes you feel the most loved?

_____

_____

_____

_____

_____

If we were created to walk in love with God, why do you think that God gave us free will in regard? In others words, why don't you think God forces us to love Him? How would that change your perspective of God? What do you learn about God's heart through the idea of free will?

_____

_____

_____

_____

SECTION 2

ESTABLISHING HEALTHY RELATIONSHIPS

Read Chapter 6

ENGAGE, REFLECT & PERSONALIZE:

How would you say that your personal relationships are impacted by your personal relationship with God? How about the opposite...how is your relationship with God impacted by your relationships with people?

_____
_____
_____
_____
_____

In the brief introduction of looking at the greatest commandment as the pattern for establishing healthy relationships, what part do you think was revelatory for you so far? Why?

_____
_____

PART 1: GOD

Read Chapter 7

ENGAGE, REFLECT & PERSONALIZE:

Think about some areas in your thinking or feeling where you know you struggle to line up with what God thinks or feels. How does the knowledge of what reconciliation looks like encourage you toward moving beyond those strongholds? Again, this concept is meant to inspire and empower you, but we first must identify those places where we are not aligning with the person of God.

_____
_____
_____
_____
_____

After reading more about your design TO BE LOVED, what have you discovered about yourself and your ability to receive love? How do you think that has affected all of your relationships?

_____
_____
_____
_____
_____

EXECUTE:

Consider John 8:32, "And you shall know the truth, and the truth shall make you free." The word, "know" in this verse means more that just having a knowledge of, but rather it is the recognition of truth by personal experience. So, it isn't just the knowledge of God that sets you free, but rather the personal experience of HIM. Spend time this week asking God to open up opportunities to really experience Him and his presence. Then do something different...worship Him in a way that is new, or go to a prayer meeting, or worship service that is "outside your box." Be willing to do something different to experience Him personally. Be sure to also pray and ask Him to show you something new, express your desire to experience His presence. It is important to note that though our relationship with God is not based on just experience; it shouldn't be just based on knowledge either. There should be a balance of both mind and heart... intellect and emotion!

Read Chapter 8

ENGAGE, REFLECT & PERSONALIZE:

Think of someone that you are convinced loves you. How do you know...in other words, how has their love for you been proven?

_____
_____
_____

A Study Guide: To Love & To Be Loved

How do you show love to people? Do you find it difficult to demonstrate love? Why or why not?

_____

_____

_____

_____

How do you show love toward God? What actions to you intentionally engage in to demonstrate love for Him? Do you find it difficult to do and/or stay intentional about?

_____

_____

_____

_____

_____

How would you say you see God demonstrate love toward people daily? How about toward you?

_____

_____

_____

How would you describe your current "season" with God? Stale, passionate, somewhere in between? Take some time to think about some of your most passionate spiritual seasons with God (honeymoon phases). What do you think cultivated that season?

_____

_____

_____

_____

28

EXECUTE:

Consider whether or not you WANT your relationship with God to be more passionate and intimate. Do you want to live in a honeymoon phase with Him forever? Consider that this is God's desire with you, and pray and thank Him for His faithful and intentional demonstrations of love for you daily. Then, ask Him to show you what you can do to live a life of demonstrating love toward Him. Expect Him to drop ideas into your heart and be prepared to put those ideas into action. Jot some of them down below as they are revealed.

_____
_____
_____
_____
_____

Read Chapter 9

ENGAGE, REFLECT & PERSONALIZE:

Are there areas in your life where you function or operate because you feel like you have to...so it feels like a "work instead of a "joy?" How would you connect this concept to Matthew 11:28-30?

_____
_____
_____
_____

What would you say you tend to tolerate or compromise? Can you see how those tolerances and/or compromises interfere with who you are called to be? How can they distract or deter you or cause you to feel like a victim?

_____
_____
_____
_____
_____

How does knowing that God is jealous for you empower you to guard your own time, energy, etc.?

_____
_____
_____
_____
_____

EXECUTE:

Take the list of tolerances and/or compromises that you made above and prayerfully consider what your life would look like if you set boundaries to guard against those. Take time to discuss this with God and consider whether or not He would find such boundaries pleasing. Remember, we set boundaries to guard our God design, NOT our "me design." This is important! Once you have established that these boundaries are pleasing to God, communicate them to those whom the boundaries may affect. Be sure to share with them that these boundaries are not about them, but rather about you guarding your own heart and putting God and His will for you first.

A Study Guide: To Love & To Be Loved

Chapter 10

ENGAGE, REFLECT & PERSONALIZE:

Was learning about the role of the priesthood, ministering to God, a new concept for you? How does this information alter the way you see yourself as a priest of the Lord? What would you say you might need to stop doing? And what would you say you might need to start doing?

_____

_____

_____

_____

How does Mary in Luke 10:38-42 demonstrate the role of a priest? Would you say that you tend to look more like Mary, or Martha in your "works"? Remember, this is not about the act itself, but rather about the heart and what our act is rooted in.

_____

_____

_____

_____

_____

Can you see any emotions in your life that tend to persuade you into doing things you don't necessarily feel are of God? For example, fear, guilt, pride, etc.

_____
_____
_____
_____
_____

EXECUTE:

Consider any activity that you are currently involved in that is not compelled out of your ministry to God first. Bring those before the Lord and ask Him if they are of the flesh or of the Spirit. Repent of the ones of the flesh and ask the Lord to direct you in cutting those things out of your life. This is part of what the act of circumcision represents...cutting away any needless flesh. Be prepared to act upon this!

Read Chapter 11

ENGAGE, REFLECT & PERSONALIZE:

Can you see how actions in your life that are rooted in the flesh are like a flame that is burning from the wick?

What are some of those actions in your life? Can you see how your "flame" is a bit smoky? Do you feel as though you "burn out" easily?

_____
_____
_____
_____

What are some ways that you keep the oil of the Holy Spirit fresh in your life? In other words, what do you do to intentionally keep your wick saturated in HIS oil...and ensure that it burns brightly and withstands any "wind"? How does His love play into that?

_____
_____
_____
_____
_____

EXECUTE:

Spend about 20 minutes just sitting in the presence of God being aware of His presence and love FOR you. Do nothing, but receive. Allow the Holy Spirit to even give you the sense of be being saturated or soaked by Him as if you were having oil poured over your whole body. Then respond prophetically thanking Him for lavishing you with His love.

"Behold what manner of love the Father has bestowed (lavished) on us, that we should be called children of God!" 1 John 3:1

Read Chapter 12

ENGAGE, REFLECT & PERSONALIZE:

After reading this part of the book, why would you say ministering to God FIRST is important? Would you say that your ministry to God IS first?

_____

_____

_____

_____

_____

What does your ministry to God look like? Do you sense how God aligns you with His heart during those times? What is the fruit (outcome)?

_____

_____

_____

_____

_____

Why do you think this is so important in establishing healthy relationships in your life? If you engaged in the love cycle with God daily, do you think it would change the way you see yourself? Do you think it would change the way you interact with others?

_____

_____

_____

_____

_____

EXECUTE:

Practice God's love for you and respond to His love. Enter into the love cycle with God by connecting with Him vulnerably and letting Him examine all of you, be transparent. Pray through Psalm 139 and let it prompt your communication with God and relish in the truth that God is familiar with all of your ways! This is not something to be ashamed of, but rather a point of connection. Remember, God wants to connect with you in your most vulnerable places.

PART 2: SELF

Read Chapter 13

ENGAGE, REFLECT & PERSONALIZE:

Be honest, how well do you love yourself? Are you in love with the story that God is telling through your life? Why or why not? Can you identify any barriers that prevent you from loving yourself?

_____

_____

_____

_____

Would you say that you struggle with the perceptions of the world? Which ones specifically? How about the perceptions of others? ... or your own perceptions of you? Does the idea of living perception free appeal to you? Why?

_____

_____

_____

_____

Describe how you think "comparison" affects the way you view yourself?

_____

_____

_____

EXECUTE:

Consider the idea of your life being a poem written by God. Now, consider that every poem reflects something about the author and His heart. If God is your author, and you are His poem, what do you think He was conveyed about Himself and His heart through your life? The purpose here is to recognize that your life holds kingdom value and is to be a display of kingdom principles. What do you think God wants to say through the way you live your life? What does your story say about God?

Read Chapter 14

Which view do you think you fall "prey" to the most...world, religion, self, or God? Why do you think that is the case?

_____
_____
_____
_____

Do you find yourself "assessing" yourself in your own head? Why do you think that is the case? How does God's view of loving yourself and His standard shatter your own view and your own standards?

_____
_____
_____
_____

A Study Guide: To Love & To Be Loved

After reading about each one, what do you think you learned the most and how do you sense God challenging you through that revelation? Do you think this revelation is an invitation to make some changes in your thoughts in regard to how you view loving yourself?

_____
_____
_____
_____

How do you think your current view has affected your relationships? How do you think your "transformed" thinking and new view of loving yourself will change that?

_____
_____
_____
_____

How do you think ministering to God first can permanently change the way you view loving yourself?

_____
_____
_____
_____
_____

EXECUTE:

Your action assignment is to pray. The way we view the idea of self-love is so important. Don't dismiss what God

38

wants to reveal to you through this chapter. Spend some time asking God to help you truly comprehend HIS heart in regard to self-love. Let Him work...and be willing to be changed. Ask Him to open your eyes to ways you love yourself according to another view. This is something God needs to reveal via the Holy Spirit. Pray daily in regard.

Make a list of standards you have for yourself. Where do these standards come from, the world, religion, yourself, or God? Make an intentional effort to release yourself from those that are not from God. This starts by recognizing them and agreeing with God that you have succumbed to other standards that are not His. Repentance may be stirred in your heart, but in the end, you should feel a sweet release from pressure that is not of God.

Read Chapter 15

ENGAGE, REFLECT & PERSONALIZE:

After reading this chapter, summarize in your own words the difference between reconciliation with God and reconciliation with self. Is this a new concept for you?

_____
_____
_____
_____
_____

A Study Guide: To Love & To Be Loved

Why do you think we often miss the step of self-reconciliation? How do you think missing that step has ultimately affected the way you love yourself?

_____
_____
_____
_____
_____

Would you say that you are challenged by truly seeing yourself through the eyes of God? In other words, do you agree with Him and extend the same love and grace to yourself that He extends toward you?

_____
_____
_____
_____

Can you think of areas in your life that are unreconciled within your own heart even though they might be reconciled with God? Remember to consider your physique, your gifts, your successes and failures, etc.

_____
_____
_____
_____
_____

EXECUTE:

Consider an area where you feel you have allowed a lie to affect the way you love yourself. Sit with the Holy Spirit and allow Him to navigate you to the moment when you first embraced that lie. Then, invite His love into that moment...wait on Him to show Himself to you in your "mind's eye" or "holy imagination." I want you to REALLY sense or see Him in that spot. Be mindful of how His presence and love begin to shift how you were feeling in that memory. Note how what He is saying is different from what you were hearing...either from a person, or in your own head. Then choose to disagree with the lie and embrace the truth of God's love and what He is saying to you. Come into agreement with Him and reconcile not just with Him, but also with you!

Read Chapter 16

ENGAGE, REFLECT & PERSONALIZE:

Be honest, when you read the title of this chapter, what was your initial reaction? Why?

_____
_____
_____
_____

Do you think it's difficult for you to consider the idea of ministering to you? Why or why not? Do you agree that it is important? Why or why not?

_____
_____
_____
_____

What do you do daily to intentionally minister to you? Consider listing spiritual, mental, emotional, and physical things. Which do you think is easiest for you? How about the hardest? Why do you think that is?

_____

_____

_____

_____

_____

Can you think of seasons where you really allowed yourself to go uncared for as a whole? How did lack of caring for one part of you spiral into not caring for the whole you?

_____

_____

_____

_____

_____

EXECUTE:

Think of one thing you can do daily to care for yourself spiritually, mentally, emotionally, and physically. Pray and ask the Lord for wisdom and creative ideas as you think. Write those things down and commit to doing them for 30 days. Then, after those 30 days, prayerfully consider what you noticed about you and how you feel.

PART 3: OTHERS

Read Chapter 17

ENGAGE, REFLECT & PERSONALIZE:

After reading this book to where you are now, are you seeing any places where you have been defined by your horizontal relationships rather than on your vertical relationship with God, or your relationship with you? How has that affected your "love-ability" toward others? How about your ability to be loved?

_____
_____
_____
_____
_____

Are there areas in your life where you know what love looks like, and you operate or act in that love, but if you were honest, it isn't truly compelled by the person of God? How can your ministry to God and self first help to spur HIS love up out of you without it feeling like an "act?"

_____
_____
_____
_____
_____

Can you see how tapping into God's person will ultimately affect the way you love others? How? What relationship do you need God's love to transform the most right now...not changing the other person, but rather changing your heart and how you love that person.

_____

_____

_____

_____

_____

EXECUTE:

Take some time to consider the list of love traits in 1 Corinthians 13:4-8. Which traits do you feel are challenging for you to receive or accept? Which ones do you feel are challenging for you to extend? Spend time receiving and agreeing with how God loves you regarding each one of these traits. Then pray in agreement with God that since He is in you, this "love-ability" is in you. Believe, receive, and release each one. Then pray about ways you can manifest those traits...even if just on faith at first. But you are operating not out of your desire to look the part, but rather to BE the part. "Faith it until you become it!"

Read Chapter 18

ENGAGE, REFLECT & PERSONALIZE:

What are areas in your life where you feel you are currently ministering to others? Would you say that you sense His holy unction in regard? Do you sense His peace and anointing while you are in that place? If not, why do you think that is the case?

_____

_____

_____

_____

Can you think of times in your life that your connection or time with God directly spurred you to minister or love on someone in a way that seemed "unusual" for you...or supernatural? Can you see how love is one of the most powerful ways we can manifest God supernaturally?

_____

_____

_____

_____

Do you think people tend to disregard His love as being the supernatural display of God? Why do you think that is?

_____

_____

_____

_____

_____

Do you see how the ministry cycle works? Have you experienced that in your own life...that your ministry to God led to ministry to man, which ultimately ministered to God? Take time to recall that account!

_____

_____

_____

_____

_____

EXECUTE:

Take inventory of where and how you are ministering to others. Are there currently any areas of ministry in your life that you need to stop doing? What has kept you from doing that thus far? Be willing to clean out the places where you are ministering out of your soul...places that are not compelled by God and His love for you.

Read Chapter 19

ENGAGE, REFLECT & PERSONALIZE:

Are there any people in your life currently that you feel unreconciled with? After reading this book, would you say that you have things that you need to reconcile first?

How can praying for your own healing and your own heart help to reconcile with that person? Do you see where that is necessary?

_____
_____
_____
_____
_____

Are there any current relationships you have that aren't currently "reconcilable" horizontally that you now realize can be reconciled within you and with God? Is that something you need to do? Do you believe that you can come to a place of total peace even though there may not be peace with you and that person?

_____
_____
_____
_____
_____

Do you think you have gained an understanding of the balance of sacrificing without sacrificing your design? Are there any places right now where you sense the Holy Spirit calling you to sacrifice? How about the opposite...are there any places where you sense Him telling you to set up some boundaries to guard your design?

_____
_____
_____
_____
_____

A Study Guide: To Love & To Be Loved

EXECUTE

Take some time to consider some of the hurts you have experienced through relationships or from specific people. Consider how God grew you through that experience and intentionally praise Him for how He worked through it to mature you.

Read the Conclusion

ENGAGE, REFLECT & PERSONALIZE:

In your own words, summarize how you see all three connections, with God, self, and others through Job's story.

_____
_____
_____
_____
_____

Do you have a Job story? Take the time to record that story down below...and then praise God for the way He is working all things out for your good and HIS glory! (Romans 8:28)

_____
_____
_____
_____

WRAPPING UP THE BOOK

PERSONALIZE:

After reading the book, what resonated with you the most and why?

_____
_____
_____
_____

Think about all the "execution" assignments. Which one or ones "worked" for you? Which one or ones do you want to continue doing? Why?

_____
_____
_____
_____

If you had to summarize this book in 1-2 sentences, what would you say?

_____
_____
_____
_____

A Study Guide: To Love & To Be Loved

If you had to summarize in 1-2 sentences how this book affected you personally, what would you say?

_____
_____
_____
_____

Please go to Amazon and write a review for the book!

You are also welcome to write a 4-5 sentence personal testimony about the book and how it impacted you and submit it through the website at www.lisa-schwarz.com.

Made in the USA
Monee, IL
21 March 2024

54854581R00026